Prayers for My

Husband

by W. Terry Whalin

Other Prayer Books by Terry Whalin

Prayers for My Son
Prayers for My Daughter
Prayers for My Wife

PRAYERS FOR MY Husband

by W. Terry Whalin

BROADMAN
&HOLMAN
PUBLISHERS

Nashville, Tennessee

© 1999 by W. Terry Whalin
All rights reserved
Printed in the United States of America

0-8054-1856-3

Published by Broadman & Holman Publishers, Nashville, Tennessee
Acquisitions & Development Editor: Vicki Crumpton
Typesetting: Desktop Services, Nashville
Page Design: Anderson-Thomas, Nashville

Dewey Decimal Classification: 242
Subject Heading: PRAYER
Library of Congress Card Catalog Number: 99-12295

Scripture quotations marked NASB are from the New American Standard Bible, © the
Lockman Foundation, 1960, 1962, 1963, 1968, 1971, 1972, 1973, 1975, 1977,
and used by permission; NIV, the Holy Bible, New International Version, © 1973,
1978, 1984 by International Bible Society; NKJV, the New King James Version, ©
1979, 1980, 1982, Thomas Nelson, Inc., Publishers; and NLT, the Holy Bible, New
Living Translation, © 1996, used by permission of Tyndale House Publishers, Inc.,
Wheaton, Illinois 60189, all rights reserved.

Library of Congress Cataloging-in-Publication Data

Whalin, Terry.
     Prayers for my husband / by W. Terry Whalin.
         p. cm.
     ISBN 0-8054-1856-3 (hardcover)
     I. Wives—Prayer-books and devotions—English. 2. Christian women—
Prayer-books and devotions—English. I. Title. II. Series: Whalin, Terry.
BV4844.W53   1999
242'.8435—dc21

99-12295
CIP

1 2 3 4 5 03 02 01 00 99

CONTENTS

Contents

Can prayer make a difference in your husband? What if your husband has no interest in spiritual matters? Throughout the centuries, wives have used prayer as a means to connect to God about their mates.

Paul Cedar, chairman of Mission America, writes in *A Life of Prayer* about counseling a young wife who had a non-Christian husband. This man militantly opposed his wife's attendance at church. Paul and his wife, Jeannie, committed to pray daily for the young husband whom they had never met. Several months later Paul greeted the wife with the encouragement, "I'm still praying every day for your husband."

She replied with astonishment and appreciation, "Oh, I have wonderful news for you. My husband came to Christ a few weeks ago. There has been a radical change in his life. In fact, he is involved in a small-group Bible study and has been attending church with me every Sunday. It's wonderful!"

Whether your husband is a Christian or not, prayer changes things. It's not a magic potent that comes with a guarantee. Instead, prayer is your opportunity to talk face-to-face with the Creator God of the universe. God invites you to communicate with him about your everyday situations and needs.

Consider for a moment the promise of I John 5:13–15: "I write this to you who believe in the Son of God, so that you may know you have eternal life. And we can be confident that he will listen to us whenever we ask him for anything in line with his will. And if we know he is listening when we make our requests, we can be sure that he will give us what we ask for" (NLT).

From these verses you know for certain that God listens to your prayers. One key is to pray for things that are within his will. And the timing for the answers to prayers? It's left in God's capable hands. Your challenge is to continue faithfully praying. God knows the beginning and the end of your days and your husband's days. The pages of this book offer you a fresh tool for prayer. Talking with God, or prayer, isn't like rubbing Aladdin's lamp with wishes. Instead, prayer is communication with the Lord of the universe. God invites you to pray for others and says in James 5:16b, "The earnest prayer of a righteous person has great power and wonderful results" (NLT).

These prayers are written in a contemporary style. Speaking to God is like talking with a best friend about a significant matter. You

Introduction

don't have to use flowery words or specific language; instead, pour out your hopes and plans to this dear friend. These prayers are written in this heart-to-heart manner. Each sample prayer points you in a fresh direction for your prayers related to your husband.

Prayer doesn't have to occur only in a particular church or place of worship. You can pray at any moment—early or late, during a coffee break or while standing in line at the grocery store. This book is designed to be carried in a briefcase or purse or to be kept at a desk in the office, then used during spare moments of time.

May God bless the prayers of your heart as you tap into this spiritual resource for your husband.

A PRAYER FOR ME

Father, thank you that through prayer I can talk with you about my husband. Before I begin praying on different topics, I ask you to touch my life.

While I can pray about my husband, I can't change him one bit. Lord, you can change my husband, but first I ask you to change me. Give me a heart full of compassion and love for my spouse. Help me to connect into your presence through prayer and reading the Bible. Give me diligence in prayer—without even the glimmer of your answer except my continued faith.

Touch my life and fill me with your Spirit. In the strong and mighty name of Jesus, amen.

"Ask and it will be given to you; seek and you will find; knock and the door will be opened to you."

MATTHEW 7:7 NIV

HIS AFFECTION

Heavenly Father, I pray for open physical affection between my husband and myself. Give us the ability to lay aside any feelings of self-consciousness so we can physically touch each other. Throughout the day, remind us to affectionately touch each other.

If a barrier has grown between my husband and myself, so that our relationship has become cold and distant, I ask you to remove the barrier. Show us how to confess our lack of affection and to change.

Thank you for your concern about this area of my relationship with my husband.

Amen.

So husbands ought also to love their own wives as their own bodies. He who loves his own wife loves himself; for no one ever hated his own flesh, but nourishes and cherishes it, just as Christ also does the church.

EPHESIANS 5:28–29 NASB

His Affection

God, it's easy to be busy. Help my husband to create time in his schedule for us to be affectionate. In the swirl of life, give us a sense of priority about physical touch. Beyond the physical, help me to develop a close relationship with my husband emotionally and spiritually. Show my husband how to lead these aspects of our relationship.

Guard his mind and relationships with others so that he will protect our marriage and not give inappropriate affection to others.

Strengthen our marriage so we don't neglect affectionate physical touch. Help us not to take each other for granted but to reach out and touch each other with affection. I commit this area of my relationship into your hands and ask for wisdom and divine insight to fill every action in my husband's day.

Amen.

Let no one seek his own, but each one the other's well-being.

I CORINTHIANS 10:24 NKJV

HIS ATTITUDE

Lord, negative information bombards my husband day in and day out. I pray that you will fill _____ with your peace. Surround him with calmness and a sense of your presence. Help his life to be God-controlled rather than circumstance- or flesh-controlled.

Enable him to live today with a clean heart, and fill him with your love and grace. Release him from anger, anxiety, inner turmoil, and pressure. If my husband is sad, help him not to be broken but to have calmness and quiet joy in the middle of this sorrow.

Shine the light of your love into his life through the power of your Spirit.

Amen.

Like a city whose walls are broken down
  is a man who lacks self-control.

PROVERBS 25:28 NIV

HIS CHOICES

Heavenly Father, I pray you will give _____ wisdom for his choices. Mold him into a man who is teachable and learns from others. Guide him to godly counselors who can give him divine insight into every decision and choice.

Give _____ strength to reject the counsel of the ungodly and to hear your voice above any other. As he rests, Lord, work in his consciousness to make wise choices rather than to follow the desires of his own flesh.

God, I understand that the wisdom of the world is foolishness with you. Help my husband not to buy into such foolish choices, but to keep his thoughts and mind focused on you and your wisdom. Grant that my husband will have ears to hear your voice.

Amen.

The fear of the LORD is the beginning of knowledge,
But fools despise wisdom and instruction.

PROVERBS 1:7 NKJV

HIS EMOTIONS

Lord, you have said that you redeem our souls when we put our trust in you. I pray for _____ that he would put his faith in you. Guard him from any negative emotions.

Protect my husband so that he is never controlled by fear, anger, depression, anxiety, jealousy, hopelessness, or suicidal thoughts. Deliver my husband from these controlling emotions. Specifically I pray for this area of concern: _____.

From reading the Bible, Lord, I know that only you can deliver and heal, but use me in the restoration process. Give me the ability to understand and encourage my husband in his struggles.

I pray for your enabling in the name of Jesus, amen.

Let your unfailing love surround us, LORD,
  for our hope is in you alone.

PSALM 33:22 NLT

HIS FATHERHOOD

God, one of the greatest potential joys of marriage is the gift of children. Assist _____ to be a good role model for his sons and daughters.

If my husband has a difficult background with his parents, I pray you will bring into his life other men who can serve as good role models for how to be a father. Drive my husband to the Bible for insight about how to father his children.

Awaken in my husband the desire to spend time with the children. Bless his efforts in those relationships, and grant him the creativity to be a fun, loving, yet wise father.

Amen.

Then Jesus was filled with the joy of the Holy Spirit and said, "O Father, Lord of heaven and earth, thank you for hiding the truth from those who think themselves so wise and clever, and for revealing it to the childlike. Yes, Father, it pleased you to do it this way."

LUKE 10:21 NLT

His Fatherhood

Lord, I pray you will give my husband balance in his fathering.

So often my husband's time is limited with the children because of other responsibilities. Help what time is available to be charged with your creative energy and blessed with your loving hand.

Grant my husband the ability to balance between a loving Heavenly Father and a Heavenly Father who desires what is right and good.

Give my husband discernment about when to discipline the children and when to lovingly forgive. It's a delicate balance, but I pray my husband will lean on you for your divine guidance.

Amen.

That the God of our Lord Jesus Christ, the Father of glory, may give to you a spirit of wisdom and of revelation in the knowledge of Him.

EPHESIANS 1:17 NASB

HIS FEARS

God, there is much in the world to fear in everyday life. I pray you will help my husband to know which fears are healthy and to discern which fears are groundless and ruling his life.

Provide my husband with a constant trust in you for the everyday events of life, and help him to understand the reality of "perfect love casts out fear." Rid my husband of any fears that are tormenting his mind and thoughts, then replace those fears with a quiet confidence in you.

Thank you, Lord, for your promises to deliver my husband from his enemies and to protect him from evil. Keep his thoughts throughout today focused on you, and supply his every need.

Amen.

For God has not given us a spirit of fear, but of power and of love and of a sound mind.

2 TIMOTHY 1:7 NKJV

HIS FINANCES

Lord, I pray you will help my husband with his finances so that he will not have any unnecessary problems. Give him wisdom to conduct his spending habits and to manage the resources from your loving hand.

Surround my husband with good role models for financial management, and provide him with good counsel in this area of his life. Give him a desire to obey your laws and also the laws of the nation regarding such matters as taxes and other required payments.

Finally, grant my husband a generous spirit—with his money, time, and talent. Financially bless my husband's resources so he can give to your work and also meet other needs in his life. Thank you in advance for your intimate interest in my husband's finances.

Amen.

"Bring all the tithes into the storehouse so there will be enough food in my Temple. If you do," says the LORD Almighty, "I will open the windows of heaven for you. I will pour out a blessing so great you won't have enough room to take it in! Try it! Let me prove it to you!"

MALACHI 3:10 NLT

His Finances

Father, I ask for you to give my husband a spirit of contentment with his finances. The message from the world says, "Get more," yet the Bible encourages us to be content. Whether in wealth or poverty, I ask for you to give _____ a gracious acceptance and satisfaction.

Give my husband and myself good communication about our finances. I pray that honesty and openness about this matter will permeate our discussions about money. Also give my husband diligence to keep good financial records and to be accountable for our finances.

Amen.

"No one can serve two masters. For you will hate one and love the other, or be devoted to one and despise the other. You cannot serve both God and money. So I tell you, don't worry about everyday life—whether you have enough food, drink, and clothes. Doesn't life consist of more than food and clothing?"

MATTHEW 6:24–25 NLT

HIS FRIENDS

God, I ask you to surround my husband with godly, male friends whom he can trust and honestly discuss any matter. May these men be wise and speak words from you, not just what my husband wants to hear. Then give my husband discernment to evaluate the advice and counsel of these friends. Help him to follow your still, small voice in these friendships.

If someone who is not a good influence tries to be my husband's friend, then I pray by the power of your Spirit to remove this person from my husband's life. Show my husband the importance of godly friendships, and help me encourage him to sustain these friendships.

Amen.

A friend loves at all times,
And a brother is born for adversity.

PROVERBS 17:17 NKJV

His Friends

Heavenly Father, help my husband learn the meaning of friendship through our relationship and also through peaceable relationships with others. Assist my husband to become a forgiving person who does not carry grudges in his heart or mind against others.

Grant my husband the grace not to judge others or hold others in contempt but to foster genuine concern in his friendships. Enable my husband to love his enemies and to bless those who curse him and to do good to those who hate him.

Finally, Lord, help me to learn how to be his best friend and grow in our friendship.

Amen.

"Therefore, if you are offering your gift at the altar and there remember that your brother has something against you, leave your gift there in front of the altar. First go and be reconciled to your brother; then come and offer your gift."

MATTHEW 5:23–24 NIV

HIS FUTURE

God, provide my husband with a vision for his future. Direct his steps in your ways, and help him understand that your plans are for good and not for evil. Grant my husband understanding of your hope for his future.

Guide _____ so he has wisdom and spiritual understanding about your will for his life. Help my husband to daily live in a manner that is pleasing to you.

May my husband not live in doubt or fear but in a quiet confidence in you, God. Assist _____ to give you his dreams and plans with the understanding that you are directing his steps.

I pray that you will grant my husband God-ordained goals for his future.

In Jesus' name, amen.

"For I know the plans I have for you," says the LORD. "They are plans for good and not for disaster, to give you a future and a hope."

JEREMIAH 29:11 NLT

HIS GRIEF AND HURTING

Lord, you know our innermost thoughts and feelings. You know the grief and hurt my husband is feeling today. I ask you to console my husband in a special way. Wipe away his tears, and restore his joy.

Grant my husband comfort. Give him a strong sense of your love and presence. Use me, Lord, to say the right words of comfort. Also give me the sensitivity to allow him space and time to heal from this situation.

Sometimes, Lord, no words suffice. Grant my husband wisdom to deal with his grief and hurting.

Amen.

Praise be to the God and Father of our Lord Jesus Christ, the Father of compassion and the God of all comfort, who comforts us in all our troubles, so that we can comfort those in any trouble with the comfort we ourselves have received from God.

2 CORINTHIANS 1:3–4 NIV

His Grief and Hurting

God, it's hard to understand your ways. My husband is wondering why _____ has happened in his life. Allow my husband to know that your ways are greater than any of us can understand. In his grief, help my husband to cast his cares on you because you care for him.

Thank you for Jesus Christ who is not a high priest unable to sympathize with our weaknesses but in all points was tempted as my husband, yet without sin. Because of Christ, my husband can boldly enter the throne of grace for mercy and help.

I thank you, God, for your provision for my husband in his time of grief.

Amen.

When you pass through the waters, I will be with you;
And through the rivers, they shall not overflow you.
When you walk through the fire, you shall not be burned,
Nor shall the flame scorch you.

ISAIAH 43:2 NKJV

19

HIS HEALTH

Father God, I pray for your healing touch on my husband. If there is anything out of balance in his physical body, set it into perfect working order. Heal _____ of any disease, injury, or weakness. Strengthen his body to successfully handle his workload, and when my husband sleeps, may he awake rejuvenated and rested.

Awaken in my husband a desire to take care of his body, eat properly, and get regular exercise. Also protect him from consuming food or drink that is harmful to him. Grant him the full awareness that his body is the temple of the Holy Spirit.

Thank you for providing my husband with health.

Amen.

Bless the LORD, O my soul,
And forget none of His benefits;
Who pardons all your iniquities;
Who heals all your diseases;
Who redeems your life from the pit;
Who crowns you with lovingkindness and compassion.

PSALM 103:2–4 NASB

His Health

Lord, touch _____'s body and restore him to health. Specifically, I pray for _____. Grant the doctors wisdom and insight as they treat my husband.

Give my husband the faith to trust you during this illness, then to follow you in health. Help my husband to follow you daily, and give him a long and healthy life. At the end of his life, give my husband peace and not unbearable suffering. Thank you, Lord, that at death you will welcome my husband into your presence—and at the appointed time—not a moment earlier.

In the mighty name of Jesus, amen.

Then your light shall break forth like the morning,
Your healing shall spring forth speedily,
And your righteousness shall go before you;
The glory of the LORD shall be your rear guard.

ISAIAH 58:8 NKJV

HIS HUMILITY

Father, whenever my husband achieves success, I pray he will always know you are the source of that success. Give my husband the ability to live in humility and turn the glory over to you.

The Bible says that pride comes before destruction. I know a proud spirit is the exact opposite of humility. Help my husband to have a humble spirit, not pride.

Surround my husband with people who will speak the truth in love. Help these friends to speak honestly to my husband, and protect him from pride. Give my husband ears to hear the loving advice from family and friends.

Thank you for how you are going to work in my husband's life in this area of humility.

Amen.

True humility and fear of the LORD lead to riches, honor, and long life.

PROVERBS 22:4 NLT

His Humility

Lord, may my husband turn to you every day of his life. I pray for the salvation of my husband, _____. In the name of Jesus, I pray you will keep him close to you throughout his life. Help my husband to live in humility and not to be puffed up with the sin of pride.

Guard my husband's steps so he will not wander away from you. Thank you, God, for your intimate interest in my husband's salvation.

Amen.

And Jesus said to him, "Today salvation has come to this house, because he also is a son of Abraham; for the Son of Man has come to seek and to save that which was lost."

LUKE 19:9–10 NKJV

HIS INTEGRITY

God, I pray you will make my husband a man of integrity who is able to stand the pressure of the world and live according to your standard. Give _____ the ability to have his yes mean yes and his no mean no.

Protect his Spirit so it doesn't waver with the pressure from society, but instead is rooted in your knowledge and wisdom. Help my husband to be teachable in spirit and listen to the voice of wisdom and instruction from your words in the Bible.

As my husband lives in integrity, then fulfill the promise of your Word, which says, "the righteous walk in integrity and his children are blessed after him" (Prov. 20:7). Provide a blessing for my children as their father walks in integrity.

In the strong name of Jesus, amen.

Let integrity and uprightness preserve me,
For I wait for Thee.

PSALM 25:21 NASB

HIS LOVE FOR OTHERS

Father, teach my husband how to fulfill the greatest commandment—to love the Lord with all his heart, soul, and mind. Then provide him with the insight to also fulfill the second commandment—to love his neighbor as himself.

Bless my husband with a love that is selfless and does not expect anything in return. Give him a generous spirit and help him to live with an open hand, willing to share with others in need through his finances, his time, and his talents.

Thank you in advance for how you are going to accomplish this love in my husband's life.

Amen.

This is love: not that we loved God, but that he loved us and sent his Son as an atoning sacrifice for our sins. Dear friends, since God so loved us, we also ought to love one another.

I JOHN 4:10–11 NIV

His Love for Others

Lord God, I ask for you to guard my husband from turning into a grumpy old man. I ask that he would have the appropriate words of encouragement and love, then speak those words in good times and bad.

If that love for others is shown through his service in the community, then open the doors for that interaction. If his love for others is shown through service in the church, then open wide those opportunities.

As my husband serves and loves other people, provide a sense of fulfillment and great joy in his life. Bless his efforts today, and I pray in the name of Jesus, amen.

Don't just pretend that you love others. Really love them. Hate what is wrong. Stand on the side of the good. Love each other with genuine affection, and take delight in honoring each other.

ROMANS 12:9–10 NLT

OUR MARRIAGE

God, I pray you will shield our marriage. Protect us from selfish attitudes, neglect, dangerous or unhealthy situations, or the evil plans and desires of others.

Remove thoughts about divorce or infidelity from our hearts—now and in the future. Set my husband free from unrealistic expectations, past hurts and memories, along with ties from previous relationships. I pray that nothing will come into our marriage that will harm it in any way. In the name of Jesus, I pray you will remove bad influences such as gambling, alcohol, drugs, pornography, lust, or obsessions.

Thank you for how Jesus celebrated marriage and performed his first miracle. I pray you will keep our marriage fresh and help us to continue to grow closer as a couple.

Amen.

Nevertheless let each individual among you also love his own wife even as himself; and let the wife see to it that she respect her husband.

EPHESIANS 5:33 NASB

Our Marriage

Lord, I pray that my husband and I will celebrate our marriage every day. Give us the desire and commitment to focus on our marriage. Eliminate immaturity, hostility, and feelings of inadequacy.

In the rush of life, give my husband a desire to make time for our marriage. Give us time alone to nurture our relationship.

I pray you will bless my husband, _____. Draw my husband close to you, Lord, so his commitment to our marriage will never fade or waiver. Help us to weather any storms in our relationship with love and commitment, which grows stronger each day. Shield us from leaving our children with a legacy of divorce. I ask for you to strengthen our marriage in Jesus' name.

Amen.

Give honor to marriage, and remain faithful to one another in marriage. God will surely judge people who are immoral and those who commit adultery.

HEBREWS 13:4 NLT

HIS OBEDIENCE

Father, you say in the Bible that if my husband cherishes sin in his heart, you will not listen. I pray my husband will live each day in obedience to you and your words in the Bible. Reveal to my husband any aspect of his life where there is sin or disobedience. Help him not to be selfish, unloving, critical, or angry. Give him a desire not to carry bitterness or resentment.

When my husband sins and disobeys your words, give him the ability to quickly turn to you for repentance and forgiveness. Provide _____ a heart and a desire to do your work and your will. Teach him your path of righteous living.

Amen.

If anyone turns a deaf ear to the law,
  even his prayers are detestable.

PROVERBS 28:9 NIV

His Obedience

Lord, awaken in my husband an obedience to your ways and your laws. Help _____ to bring every thought and action under your control. Remind him to do good and to speak evil of no one. Help _____ to be peaceable, gentle, and humble in his everyday life.

Drive my husband to turn to your words in the Bible every day, and increase his understanding from those hours of study. Give him the insight and ability to hear your still, small voice, then enable him to obey your words.

Finally, provide _____ the peace that only comes from living in obedience to you and your commands.

Amen.

"Observe and obey all these words which I command you, that it may go well with you and your children after you forever, when you do what is good and right in the sight of the LORD your God."

DEUTERONOMY 12:28 NKJV

His Other Relatives

God, thank you for my husband's relatives. I ask for you to bless our ties to extended family such as siblings, cousins, aunts, and uncles. We may see these relatives often or rarely, but I pray for your hand to guide and bless our relationships with them.

Give my husband the desire and energy to maintain these family relationships—even if rarely. Use my husband as a source of encouragement and strength to other family members. Mold him into an example of strength so that others in the family can turn to him and confide in him with confidence.

If anger or resentment or hard feelings exist in these relationships, then I ask you, God, for your healing touch to minister within my husband's family. I express my own availability to be used as an instrument of peace. Help me have the right words so I can sow peace where there is discord.

In your strong and mighty name, amen.

For the sake of my brothers and my friends,
I will now say, "May peace be within you."

PSALM 122:8 NASB

HIS PARENTS

God, thank you for _____'s parents. I pray you will bless the relationship between my husband and his parents. Help it to grow from an adult-to-child relationship into an adult-to-adult relationship. Give my husband a desire to honor his parents. If there is pain and disruption in this relationship, heal the old wounds by the power of your Spirit.

As my husband's parents grow older, I pray you will help us to make wise decisions about their health care and how to support and encourage them. Bless my relationship with my in-laws and our communication with one another.

I pray for your blessing on my husband's parents and this important relationship for my husband.

Amen.

"Honor your father and your mother, that your days may be prolonged in the land which the LORD your God gives you."

EXODUS 20:12 NASB

HIS PAST

Heavenly Father, I pray for _____ to completely release his past. Deliver my husband from any hold that the past may have on his life. Give my husband the strength and ability to put off the old nature and to embrace a new life, which is centered on you.

Thank you that your steadfast love never ceases and your mercies never come to an end but are new every morning. Give my husband ears to listen to your voice. Quiet the voices and thoughts of his past life, and enable him to hear the truth of your words.

Amen.

Therefore, if anyone is in Christ, he is a new creation; old things have passed away; behold, all things have become new.

2 CORINTHIANS 5:17 NKJV

His Past

Lord, I pray for healing in my husband's life from his past. Take the old hurts and heal them by the power of your Spirit. Touch his innermost thoughts and cleanse them from the impurities of the past.

Help my husband to see his past as a history lesson and not a guide for daily life. If his past has any unpleasant memories, I pray you will redeem his thoughts and purify them with the power of your Word.

Give my husband the ability to restore his soul as he releases his past into your capable hands. Lead my husband to your future plans for his life.

Amen.

Therefore we do not lose heart. Though outwardly we are wasting away, yet inwardly we are being renewed day by day. For our light and momentary troubles are achieving for us an eternal glory that far outweighs them all.

2 CORINTHIANS 4:16–17 NIV

HIS PEACE

Father God, I pray that my husband will have the peace that passes all understanding. Life gets hectic at times, and I pray you will empower my husband with your peace. In the midst of constant change, provide my husband with calmness and confidence in you and your presence in his life.

Lord, when turmoil enters my husband's life, provide him with the communication skills to be a peacemaker. Jesus told us that blessed are those who work for peace for they will see God. In the middle of strife, grant my husband a sense of clarity in his speech and the ability to calm the situation. Fill my husband's life with peace today.

Amen.

You will keep in perfect peace all who trust in you,
whose thoughts are fixed on you!

ISAIAH 26:3 NLT

HIS PRIORITIES

Lord, be the ruler of my husband's life today. Order his steps, and show him how to set you ahead of everything else. In the rush of life, it's difficult to know which tasks should come first. Quiet my husband's spirit, and help him to turn to you—not to the loudest, most demanding voice.

Speak to my husband about his priority of spending time with you, reading the Bible, and prayer. Enable _____ to place a greater prominence on me and our children than he does on work, friends, or other activities.

Grant my husband the ability to seek you first, then I know you will order the other pieces of his life in a perfect arrangement.

Thank you for your interest in this important area of my husband's life.

Amen.

Let each of you look out not only for his own interests, but also for the interests of others.

PHILIPPIANS 2:4 NKJV

HIS PROTECTION

Father God, I pray your protection on _____. Shield him from any accidents, diseases, dangers, or the influence of evil. Especially protect him when he travels in a car or airplane.

Keep my husband on your path so that his foot does not slip. If he does slip and fall, I pray you will restore him through your mercy. Even when bad things happen to my husband, I pray he will cast his cares on you, then live in your protective hand. Preserve my husband from his enemies.

I ask for his protection in the powerful name of Jesus.

Amen.

The LORD is my rock, my fortress and my deliverer;
my God is my rock, in whom I take refuge.
He is my shield and the horn of my salvation, my stronghold.
I call to the LORD, who is worthy of praise,
and I am saved from my enemies.

PSALM 18:2–3 NIV

HIS PURPOSE

Lord, I pray that my husband will sense your calling and purpose on his life. Guide his steps so he can sense your loving hand in his decisions—large and small. Continually remind my husband of his purpose, and don't allow him to be sidetracked into nonessentials.

During those moments when through circumstances he questions your purpose, remind him of your design on his life. Then help him cling to those plans. Thank you that your timing is perfect and never off or out of sync. Give my husband patience to wait on your timing for his plans.

I thank you for how you are going to direct the purpose of my husband's life.

Amen.

To this end also we pray for you always that our God may count you worthy of your calling, and fulfill every desire for goodness and the work of faith with power.

2 THESSALONIANS 1:11 NASB

HIS REPUTATION

Heavenly Father, I pray my husband will have a reputation that is untarnished. I ask that other people will speak highly of him and that he will be respected in our community and in his workplace. Protect him from lawsuits and entanglements. Guard his reputation so that he will be known for his honesty, trustworthiness, and humility in each of his dealings with others.

Preserve my husband from his enemies or those who would harm him. Keep him away from gossiping people who would harm his reputation with false accusations and words. If others do try to harm my husband's reputation, then, God, I ask for you to execute your justice and mighty hand. Lead my husband so that his decisions are wise and his reputation without fault.

Amen.

Choose a good reputation over great riches, for being held in high esteem is better than having silver or gold.

PROVERBS 22:1 NLT

HIS SELF-IMAGE

Lord, in a world that tries to mold my husband's self-image, I pray
_____ will find his confidence and identity in you. Give my husband
understanding to appreciate his value and worth in your eyes.

Help my husband to understand his unique abilities and talents.
Then bring others into his life that can affirm these qualities. Use me
in this affirmation process in his life.

Provide my husband with a peace and security because he rests in
the knowledge of your acceptance and love. Free _____ from a focus
on self so that he can focus his attention on you.

Restore his confidence in you today.

Amen.

*Do not lie to one another, since you have put off the old man with his deeds, and
have put on the new man who is renewed in knowledge according to the image of
Him who created him.*

COLOSSIANS 3:9–10 NKJV

His Sexuality

Father, I pray you will bless my husband's sexuality and fulfill his needs in this area of his life. Give our marriage a sense of balance. Provide time in the busyness of life for open communication and sensitivity to each other's needs.

Help my husband to flee anything illicit or lustful. Deliver my husband from any sins in his past. Remove anything or anyone who would tempt my husband into immorality.

Show me how to be a good sexual partner for my husband. I ask for you to bless this aspect of my husband's life.

Amen.

Let the husband fulfill his duty to his wife, and likewise also the wife to her husband. The wife does not have authority over her own body, but the husband does; and likewise also the husband does not have authority over his own body, but the wife does.

I CORINTHIANS 7:3–4 NASB

HIS SPEECH

God, I know words can hurt or heal. I pray as my husband speaks today that you will guard his mouth and his words. Assist him not to be a complainer or grumbler or someone who uses foul language or speaks words to hurt and destroy others.

Guide my husband in the path of righteous actions and speech. Fill him with your love and Spirit so that his speech builds up others and doesn't tear them down.

Bless my communication with my husband today. Show us how to encourage and respect each other as we share our feelings and words. I ask that the words of my husband's mouth and the meditations of his heart will be acceptable in your sight, Lord.

Amen.

"A good person produces good words from a good heart, and an evil person produces evil words from an evil heart."

MATTHEW 12:35 NLT

His Spiritual Development

HIS SPIRITUAL DEVELOPMENT

Lord, I pray you will draw my husband into a deeper relationship with you. Give _____ a desire to turn to you daily through prayer and to read and study the Bible. Thank you for the many opportunities you have provided for my husband's spiritual growth—through the Bible, prayer, good books, and teaching from pastors and others.

Help my husband to lead our family to a Bible-based church, and bless his leadership in our home. Guide me in how to encourage _____ in his spiritual development. Remind my husband of your presence throughout this day, and give him an unquenchable desire to grow in the knowledge of you.

Amen.

For this reason we also, since the day we heard it, do not cease to pray for you, and to ask that you may be filled with the knowledge of His will in all wisdom and spiritual understanding.

COLOSSIANS 1:9 NKJV

HIS STRENGTH

God, I pray you will help my husband to live on the solid rock of confidence in you. If he requires inner strength, I pray my husband will turn to you. If my husband feels weak, I pray he will find his strength from you. Thank you that you have chosen to pour out your goodness and kindness on the weak vessels.

Help my husband to cast his hopes on you so you will restore his strength. Base my husband's confidence on the truth in your words. Thank you that when we are weak you are strong, so I ask for your strength in my husband's life today.

Amen.

But those who hope in the LORD
will renew their strength.
They will soar on wings like eagles;
they will run and not grow weary,
they will walk and not be faint.

ISAIAH 40:31 NIV

His Temptations

Father, give my husband the strength and skills to resist temptation. Lead him not into temptation but deliver him from such evils as alcohol, drugs, food addictions, gambling, adultery, and pornography. Remove the temptations especially in the area of _____.

Establish a wall of protection around my husband. Give _____ the ability to take charge of his spirit and to have the self-control to resist anything or anyone who lures him into evil. I pray my husband will be repulsed by tempting situations. Teach him to live today in the power of your Spirit to overcome evil.

In the mighty name of Jesus, amen.

No temptation has seized you except what is common to man. And God is faithful; he will not let you be tempted beyond what you can bear. But when you are tempted, he will also provide a way out so that you can stand up under it.

I Corinthians 10:13 NIV

His Temptations

Lord God, guard my husband from temptations. The Bible says my husband should avoid the works of the flesh: adultery, fornication, uncleanness, lewdness, idolatry, sorcery, hatred, contentions, jealousies, outbursts of wrath, selfish ambitions, dissensions, heresies, envy, murders, drunkenness, revelries, and the like (Gal. 5:19). Shield my husband from each of these evil works. I especially ask you, Lord, to remove the area of _____.

I ask that you will grant my husband a measure of courage to resist evil.

In your powerful name, amen.

Let no one say when he is tempted, "I am tempted by God"; for God cannot be tempted by evil, nor does He Himself tempt anyone. But each one is tempted when he is drawn away by his own desires and enticed. Then, when desire has conceived, it gives birth to sin; and sin, when it is full-grown, brings forth death.

JAMES 1:13–15 NKJV

THANKSGIVING FOR HIM

Lord God, thank you for my husband. In thanksgiving for his life, I want to thank you for bringing us together. Your ways of leading are mysterious.

I praise you for the skills and talents you have created in my husband from birth. I thank you for our marriage and our family life. I want to express appreciation to you, Heavenly Father, for my husband's commitment to our family and his love for family. Also, thank you for my husband's work and the creative energy he pours into his occupation.

There is much to be grateful for in my husband's life. Awaken in me the ability to recount my thanksgiving, and to express it to you in prayer and also to my husband.

In appreciation for your provision, amen.

I will give thanks to Thee, O Lord my God, with all my heart,
And will glorify Thy name forever.

PSALM 86:12 NASB

HIS TIMES OF REFRESHMENT

Heavenly Father, sometimes it's difficult to relax. I pray for your provision in this area of my husband's life. Give him the ability to escape his work and worries, then to have times of refreshment and renewal.

I pray that you will bless my husband's hobbies. If he doesn't have a hobby, I pray you will provide something that he enjoys and gives him a sense of accomplishment and spiritual renewal.

When my husband plays with friends or the family, I pray you will use this time to rebuild and restore his physical body and emotional soul. Create in my husband a balanced approach to his life. I ask you to provide times of refreshment for my husband.

Amen.

Then wonderful times of refreshment will come from the presence of the Lord, and he will send Jesus your Messiah to you again.

ACTS 3:20 NLT

HIS TRIALS

Lord, you know the burden my husband is carrying. I pray for him especially in the area of _____. Strengthen my husband and provide him with faith in you.

Give my husband joy in the midst of this difficulty so when others look at his situation, it will testify to your involvement in his life. Thank you that you didn't come to remove such trials from my husband's life, but you allow us to come boldly into the throne of your grace. I place this situation into your capable hands.

Amen.

In this you greatly rejoice, even though now for a little while, if necessary, you have been distressed by various trials, that the proof of your faith, being more precious than gold which is perishable, even though tested by fire, may be found to result in praise and glory and honor at the revelation of Jesus Christ.

I PETER 1:6–7 NASB

His Trials

God, you are my husband's refuge and strength, a very present help in times of trouble. You know the details of my husband's difficulty. Keep him close to you during this situation so he's able to run with endurance the race you have set before him. Build and strengthen my husband's faith and love of you, so that no matter what the outcome of this situation, he will be stronger in his relationship with you.

I thank you for how you use trials to build character into my husband. When my husband cries out to you, hear his prayer and deliver him from his troubles.

In the strong name of Jesus, amen.

Consider it pure joy, my brothers, whenever you face trials of many kinds, because you know that the testing of your faith develops perseverance.

JAMES 1:2–3 NIV

HIS WISDOM

Father God, you've said that the fear of the Lord is the beginning of wisdom. I pray you will bless my husband with a desire to acquire your wisdom and to walk in your ways. Give him a thirst for more knowledge about you and to read the Bible.

In his family, work, and other activities, bless him with a hunger for your wisdom. Bless my husband with the ability to learn and increase his wisdom. Each day my husband is bombarded with information, yet I pray you will give him discernment about your ways and your desires. Help him to seek you and your wisdom for whatever he needs today.

Amen.

Wisdom is the principal thing;
Therefore get wisdom.
And in all your getting, get understanding.
Exalt her, and she will promote you;
She will bring you honor, when you embrace her.

PROVERBS 4:7–8 NKJV

HIS WORK

Lord, I pray you will bless the work of my husband's hands. Give him a vision for his work and a sense of fulfillment. May his work bring prosperity and a provision for the needs of our family. If my husband's work is outside of your plans for his life, I pray you will remove his work and replace it with something you desire. Keep my husband close to you in his work, and help his thoughts to frequently turn to you and your plans for his occupation.

Give my husband confidence in the specific talents and abilities you have given him. Now bless those abilities, and strengthen him so his work is successful, satisfying, and financially rewarding.

Thank you for your loving hand.

Amen.

Do you see any truly competent workers? They will serve kings rather than ordinary people.

PROVERBS 22:29 NLT

His Work

Lord God, I pray you will protect my husband from laziness. Motivate him today with his work so that he is a diligent worker and not one who cuts corners and looks for the easy way out. I pray you will give him a sense of pride in his work and a desire to work with excellence.

May _____ never run from work out of fear, selfishness, or a desire to avoid responsibility. On the other hand, give my husband balance so that he doesn't overwork or drive himself unnecessarily. Give my husband a balance so he has the right amount of work without being overworked.

Be the Lord of my husband's work, and help him to bring each aspect of his occupation under your control.

Amen.

If a man is lazy, the rafters sag;
* if his hands are idle, the house leaks.*

ECCLESIASTES 10:18 NIV

His Worries

Lord, you know the worries my husband is facing. I pray specifically for _____. For these concerns, I pray you will enable my husband to cast his cares on you. Thank you for the provision you have made for us through Jesus Christ to talk with you about our cares.

If my husband thinks long enough about his burden, it can consume his thinking. I pray you will guard him from this type of anxiety. Give him the freedom to release his cares into your hands—not to take them back but to thoroughly release them.

Thank you for caring for my husband and his worries.

Amen.

Anxiety in the heart of a man weighs it down,
But a good word makes it glad.

PROVERBS 12:25 NASB

His Worries

Lord, you've declared in the Bible that worry is a sin. I pray for my husband and his concerns or worries. Give him the ability to release these worries into your care. Your shoulders are broad, and you can carry these concerns with far more grace and capacity than my husband.

Use me to work with my husband as a sounding board. Help me to listen to _____'s concerns. Give my husband creative ideas from your guiding hand to release him from these worries.

Today my husband needs your touch in his life to release his worries. I pray he will turn to you with an honest and open heart.

Amen.

Therefore humble yourselves under the mighty hand of God, that He may exalt you in due time, casting all your care upon Him, for He cares for you.

I Peter 5:6–7 NKJV

ABOUT THE AUTHOR

W. Terry Whalin is the author of more than fifty books, including *The Book of Prayers, A Man's Guide to Reaching God*. He has also coauthored many books, including *First Place* and *Lessons from the Pit* (Broadman & Holman), as well as numerous biographies, which include *Chuck Colson* and *Luis Palau*. The former editor at *Decision* and *In Other Words*, Terry is a full-time freelance journalist and lives with his wife, Christine, in Colorado Springs, Colorado. You can learn more about Terry's work at www.terrywhalin.com.